AS ABOVE

SO IS BELOW

LADY SHELBY KELLAM

Books may be ordered on Amazon or by contacting:
Lady Shelby Kellam at email:
shelbykellam1@gmail.com
1 (336) 497-1737

ISBN-13: 978-0-9983404-3-2
Library of Congress Control Number: 2018913904
Printed in the United States of America

Table of Contents

Dedicated

This book is dedicated to my wonderful family. To my beautiful parents that imparted wisdom and taught me to never give up. To always soar and count the cost. You have taught me how to work hard with integrity and respect.

To my sons in whom I couldn't be more proud of I love you and thank you for always loving me, for believing in me, and encouraging me. You are and will always be my why.

To my grandson Zaiden, you are truly Gigi's heart. You are truly special and an amazing young man. I can't wait to see your future unfold.

To my dearest husband; Bishop Reginald B. Kellam, the love of my life. You are my biggest fan, supporter, and my best friend. You inspire me to be a better woman, wife, and mother. I love you and thank you for all of your support, love, and most of all your prayers.

To every person that reads this book, I thank you for your love and support.

Preface

Level up and be the expressive gift of God. Take the time to adhere to his unveiling truth. Levels can be hard to climb as each round goes higher and higher. But it can be a teachable moment as we embark on new and different territories of our life. Each path we travel has its own turns and oppositions. We have the power to achieve, conquer, and make the best out of life. It is given in hopes that one may examine themselves in order to balance out the necessities to obtain victory on each level you have to encounter. It's ok to be free. Free to be you and soar like your why depended on it. Don't forget why you started. The how cannot be greater than the why. As you make a decision to level above any breaks of life, remember to just keep moving and believe it. If you find yourself below a point of place in life, don't quit but do as time does keep moving. Take the time to heal and be restored. No matter what life brings you are equipped to transition and make great decisions. You don't owe your past an apology as much as you owe your future an opportunity. Always be inspired and live your best life remembering the first change comes from within. Because no matter where life may take you, you will always carry yourself wherever you go. A change can come and I pray it does. But examine yourself and make the necessary changes; starting with you, your heart, mind, body, and soul. Remember this time you win!

SUCCESS ISN'T JUST ABOUT WHAT YOU ACCOMPLISH IN YOUR LIFE. IT'S ABOUT WHAT YOU INSPIRE OTHERS TO DO.

CHAPTER 1

You Don't Owe Your Past an Apology As Much As You Owe Your Future an Opportunity

Have you ever wondered what on earth you were here to do? Have you just pondered to think what you have done thus far? And what is it that you need to get done? Well, how old are you? How many years have went by? How many resolutions have we made; have we fulfilled it; any of these, all of these, or none of these? And is life coming? Are we prepared? Are we prepared to give it back to our kids so that they can be prepared? Because what you do now is going to reflect you for the rest of your life. And as time comes in we have to be ready and we have to be prepared.

So how do we get prepared? I'm so glad you asked. As I think of how I came to the realization of knowing what I was called to do, it kind of scared me to the point I asked myself; how will I be able to do all of this? And what is all of this? In being prepared you have to do your research. Ask yourself what is it that you're trying to aim for? Do I have the necessary tools to get this accomplished? Do I have the skill set? Do I have the mindset? Is my body prepared to handle what all needs to be done? Because you have to line up everything that you're going to be involved in; in order to get a great outcome. You've got to be able to put in some time. You are going to need some time. Time is very valuable. And it is something you can never get back.

You may find yourself in seasons where it may seem insurmountable, but you just have to keep chipping at it in bits and pieces and before you know it you are finished at what you thought you couldn't achieve. Maximize the moment by starting out with a prayer to command your day; your words have power to bring life or death. Then strategize and execute the plan. I will say you must start somewhere or you will find yourself stuck in the same place you were the year before. Just get started. It doesn't matter how fast you run. This race is not given to the swift, neither to the strong. But to the one that endures to the end. You have got to get up and start doing something. You can't just sit still, because if you do, you won't do anything. You have got to make a conscious decision that, hey, this is where I may be, but this is where I am going to be. That's what I did. I posted my dreams up. And prepared my vision board, so that I could have a clear visual of what I see come into a reality.

Now, I encourage you today to do the same, just get up and start where you are at. Apply what you have; your degree, your knowledge, your skill set, and your gift and use it to the best of your ability. Your gift will make room for you. And it will work if you work it.

NOTES

NOTES

NOTES

NOTES

_____

_____

_____

_____

_____

_____

_____

_____

_____

_____

_____

_____

_____

_____

_____

_____

_____

_____

_____

_____

_____

_____

_____

_____

_____

"FOR THE WEAPONS OF OUR WARFARE ARE NOT CARNAL, BUT MIGHTY THROUGH GOD TO THE PULLING DOWN OF STRONGHOLDS; CASTING DOWN IMAGINATIONS AND EVERY HIGH THING THAT EXALTETH ITSELF AGAINST THE KNOWLEDGE OF GOD BRINGING INTO CAPTIVITY EVERY THOUGHT TO THE OBEDIENCE OF CHRIST."

CHAPTER 2

Road Construction Ahead

"My flesh and my heart faileth: but God is the strength of my heart, and my portion forever."

~~~Psalm 73:26~~~

As you travel there may be times when you see a sign ahead that will say Road Construction Ahead. That's what happens in our life when we're traveling, and we come against something that is considered one lane above or a road construction. So that means your route is going to be altered.

What happens when you are traveling along the highway and your route becomes altered? What do you do? What I did was as I was traveling, my life became altered I realized that either I can alter my life to go around what is going to be ahead of me and I can get through it by altering it or I can turn around and go back and wait until the construction is over, which there is not an estimate time of when it may be complete. So what I did; I'm not saying what you need to do, but this is what I always do. I never let any obstacle defeat me.

Defeat is not an option. Whatsoever a man thinks, so is he. I think it in my mind. I can do it, and so I get it done.

Have you ever filled out a resume that asks you what your strengths and weaknesses are? My weakness is completing something and not enough time to finish it. In other words, if you give me a project to get done and if it's already twelve o'clock, instead of going to bed, I'm going to get it completed. Because I am not going to bed until it is done. And that to me is a good weakness to have. But I realize that everyone does not think that way. So I am trying to give you some principles and ideas to shape your mindset to let you see that your mindset is what's going to drive your determination.

If your mind set is not clear, and if you don't have pure thoughts, then your determination is going to be slothful, you're not going to care less what you do, you are just going to shoot at life aimlessly. You hit or miss; if I do I do, if I don't, I don't. Well, that's not the attitude to have, because you fail, and have to start over again and again. It's okay to fail at something because it is in the failing that you may learn what to do and what not to do. It may take some of us failing in order to be redirected to where destiny has been awaiting our arrival. Don't question the process, as much as you learn the lesson. For if you learn the lesson then your process can be completed for you to be able to start another journey in your life. And I don't know about you, but sometime I don't have the time to keep starting over and over; because consistency is what you want to have done in your life. You want to be able to be consistent. Even though your pattern may be altered or it may change; it does not justify that it's going to always be that way.

You have to see yourself where you are going in the beginning. You have to see the ending in the beginning. Because if you don't see where you are going, you will never know how to get there. A GPS is good to have. It will give you the route, but it will only speak when you are going in the wrong direction. And sometimes in our life we need to do a U-turn.

NOTES

NOTES

NOTES

LADY SHELBY KELLAM

NOTES

_____

_____

_____

_____

_____

_____

_____

_____

_____

_____

_____

_____

_____

_____

_____

_____

_____

_____

_____

_____

_____

_____

IF YOU NEVER HEAL FROM WHAT HURT YOU, YOU'LL BLEED ON PEOPLE WHO DIDN'T CUT YOU.

CHAPTER 3

What's Next?

Now that you have kind of figured out some things in your life and it is heading in the right direction. What happens when you get that curve ball? What happens when what you planned really doesn't plan out the way you planned; what do you do now? Do you stop or do you keep going? What do you ask yourself? Why is this happening to me or do you ask yourself; what is next, now that this has happened to me? Yes, that's what I did, I said ok, what's next because I realized that even though it didn't pan out the way I wanted it, I was not going to allow it to defeat me. Because I believe in myself and when it gets to a point where you stop believing in yourself then that's the point where you're going to stop doing, you're going to stop caring and you're going to stop believing. You must get up. You must understand that things may not happen the way you orchestrate them to be. But in time, give anything time. And I promise you, it will work out for your good.

And now that you have grown up and are becoming more mature while doing this thing called life, you are on the right track picking up the pieces of yourself and putting them together, you're on the right road now. As you continue to grow, it's going to be interesting to you to discover that you can live your best life. You just have to get up and then show up. After you get up and show up, you are ready for whatever life throws at you. You will find that what should have killed you, only made you stronger, and now you're just a testimony to saying I was created for something, I don't know exactly what all. But I do know I was created for something. I can handle this. Bring it on! Because when you stop and don't count the cost of what took you years to build and come through, can take you minutes to lose it all, including yourself. Someday you will realize that all of what you are doing comes with a high price. And you must realize that it is essential to have all your priorities in order. That was the one thing I had to do.

So, now you will know that life's journey is going to come through different paths. It's going to come in different strengths. Sometimes you're going to be up; sometimes you're going to be down. But as above so is below. You never know how you're going to be. But you've got to make the best of whatever you are. You've got to make the best of where you're at. You know sometimes when you say to yourself, life is going to come; ready or not here it comes; that's what life can do to you, life picked us up and grew us up, and sometimes we were ready and sometimes we weren't; but sometimes you have to ask the Lord to show you the missing pieces of yourself. Because whatever's missing, that's what you're going to have to fix. We can search the world all over, and for some of us, we've been around the world three times and spoke to everybody twice. We will have both high and low days. Sometimes we will try to fix our problems. But fixing our problem sometimes, whatever the ailment may be, can only come through a spiritual walk with Christ. Become a new creature and dismantle the old man.

Remember now, while you are working on you, allow others to grow as you did. Don't get self-righteous and think that your short comings weren't as big as others. We have all sinned and come short of God's glory. It's only by his grace and Mercy that we are here today; and not consumed. The same God that forgave you will be the same God that forgives your oppressors. Yes, I know they did you wrong and hurt your heart. But one thing you must come to peace with is this: Make peace with all men and if they continue to do you wrong, God will be your vindicator. I have seen him do it; not that you get a thrill on seeing others get a taste of their own medicine. How you will know that you have grown mature is when you have the opportunity to do someone dirty but you choose not to. When others come back to you to ask for forgiveness, you must accept so your blessings will not be hindered. Now you may have some that may never come back and ask for your forgiveness because they are still practicing the wrong, or have not learned their lesson. Two wrongs don't make a right, or, does it?

I've noticed that I have a peace that surpasses all understanding, even when you had to question life in general and ask yourself how did it all start? What part did you say and do or didn't say or do to make your life better or bitter? Because we can never fix our own life until we realize there is something that definitely needs to be fixed. Once you fix the missing part of you, then you will never allow others to put you in a situation where you are a victim of their circumstances. You cannot make people do anything, but you do have the power to choose how you will allow others to do unto you.

When you find people that want to blast your mistakes and your short comings, I promise you they are covering up their own. We can see the visible signs or the wrong in a person; but what about the inward things that cannot be seen such as matters of the heart that filters love, hate, jealousy, envy and malice, just to name a few. Before we try to get the splinter out of our neighbor's eye, we must get the two by four out of our own. People want to be real and keep it one hundred until it comes to their address. If we would focus as much time on our short comings and mastering them, then and only then can we start to understand the shortcoming of others. Whether we want to admit it or not, we all have had a wild moment where we can say I can't believe I did or said that.

Show compassion toward others because it's only by the grace of God, woah goes I. I don't know what your struggle may have been. But don't allow the weaknesses of others to keep you trapped in a cycle of losing your identity. I realize that even though life has come, and ready or not. Sometimes you're prepared and sometimes you're not. You have to make the best with what you have. You have to learn how to make it. You have to learn how to survive. You have to learn how not to compare your life to anyone else's. But encourage yourself, you know, hey this is where I am; realistically I don't even know how I got here. But I'm going to deal with where I am at. You know I'm not going to try to be no more than I am. I'm not trying to do no more than I can do. I'm going to pick up the pieces of where I'm at. And then I'm going to just repair where I'm at and try to figure it out.

Sometimes life can cause you to have a setback. When that happens we get to a point where we don't even want to try again, because we compete and we compare. The only person you should compete with is your own self or what you did yesterday. And that's the only person. Because trust and believe the rest of you should be the best of you. There's got to be times in your life that you say you know what, I have to stay focused. I have to keep my mind on what I'm thinking and doing because it's so much around me, and people are doing a lot of things; some good, some bad, some indifferent. But until you can decide what is right for you, you cannot partake in everything. And if you don't keep your eyes on what you're doing, you'll be wrapped up and get caught up in stuff that you had no business getting caught up in.

Another season in your life will cause you to change courses and start all over again. Getting new friends won't change if you haven't done the maintenance on you. Remember that you will take yourself wherever you go. Prayer is your secret weapon so let's stop where we are and pray.

"I pray for God to remove every toxic and hindering spirit from around you and your family that mean you no good. Private haters and fake celebrators will be exposed right now, in Jesus' name."

People want to know what you are doing because they are curious to know and grow to better themselves. But when you show them, they can't handle it and they start judging you. What took you years to build the enemy thinks can be done overnight. Stay focused and when you have put your time in, then and only then can you or will you be prepared and ready to stand the attacks of the enemy.

Our heart, sometimes has to remind us, sugar, you're here for a heartbeat and to pump blood and not to put your heart into everything that's around you; even though sometimes that's hard to do especially when you have a great heart. Never allow anyone to mistreat you based on their inability to see your value. Some people have judged you based on what their family members or associates have said about you or people in general that was not true. They could be the one to send you a friend request on Facebook and don't like anything you do. They just want to keep up with what you are doing. Go figure, I know we have all been there.

NOTES

NOTES

NOTES

NOTES

YOU CAN'T BE WHO GOD CALLED YOU TO BE AND STILL KEEP ALL THE SAME FRIENDS AND HABITS. ELEVATIONS REQUIRE SEPARATION.

CHAPTER 4

Living Your Best Life

The kings heart is in the hand of the Lord, as the rivers of water, he turneth it withersoever he will.

Let your OBSERVATION take precedence over your EXPECTATION period. In other words, go with the flow. Some would say not to have any expectations at all. But I would not go that far. I think healthy, realistic expectations that are communicated are good to have. They're something to reach for. But when you come into a situation and your expectations aren't met, let your observation take the lead. Discard your expectation in the moment and deal with the reality at hand. If you are tired of being frustrated, set aside your unmet expectations and face reality head on. Then after the fact, have a conversation with whoever is involved about what you expect and why.

When you want to grow in life, it will start when we decide to let go of what we think defines us. It was in my weakness that I found my divinity. When your weakness is exposed that's when God shows you strength. When the heart begins to take the lead the eyes will follow.

I'm sorry to say but you must detach yourself from all distractions and people that take life as a joke. Listen to me; they will never be able to value you because they don't value themselves. Let them keep on laughing, judging, and criticizing your life. The only person that will be distracted by the noise will be the ones with a weak mind and people that always cry the victim. You must continue to focus and keep winning. You will thank me later. No more wasting your time is the mindset that you have to have in order to reach your goals. You can continue to open your crackerjack box and get your prize, or press toward the mark for the prize of the high calling of God in Christ Jesus.

We are here to serve, love and bless others in the process. It's only when we don't know who we are and how valuable we are that we downsize others. You don't need someone to tell you who you are or not. We all should be mirroring our Heavenly Father. People are different and you will come to a season in your life that you will turn off all negative and immature actions from people, places, or things that may have not been exposed, or were brought up with a vindictive mentality. You see people's demeanor and the looks they secretly give you. Stop giving in to that controlling, manipulative spirit because you are merely wasting time and energy. Go get your life and stop allowing others with a closed mind that can't see the bigger you.

Sometimes you have to constantly remind yourself that you have come to the conclusion that some people were just raised differently. Some people were truly raised different and so when you come around them or they come around you, they may not understand your concept or the way you think or do things. It's not that you are trying to embark or imply your thoughts on them. But the question is can you come to some common ground where you both can reason and agree? Because if you both are a good person with a good heart, there should be nothing you can't work out. Remember you are living your best life. And it starts with you.

NOTES

NOTES

NOTES

NOTES

BETTER GET YOU A FRIEND
THAT CAN PRAY YOU
THROUGH YOUR MESS
INSTEAD OF ONE THAT
KEEPS YOU IN THE MESS.

CHAPTER 5

Life's Lesson

Keep being the Masterpiece that you are. If anyone questions about how God has designed you, tell them to take it up with the Master Designer, God himself, for it is He that has made us, and not we our-selves.

Sometimes it's good for you to see people's true colors. Remember everyday of your life you have the victory!! Stay Woke!!! You are becoming a better you, trust the process!! Let your spiritual man discern and not your intellect, because your intellect will have you questioning everything, but your spiritual man will allow you to let others be who they are while allowing God to mold and shape them.

Peoples' character will expose their integrity! But don't quit because it's building you. Will you be able to handle what God is about to reveal? Can you handle it when He shows you? Don't let it catch you off guard. There is only a remnant of people that truly want the best for you, with no hidden agenda. When God shows you take heed. When peoples character isn't right they will do whatever they think and want to do and forget how you feel because they are all for themselves! You must stay awake and have a keen discernment. And don't let it stop you from loving.

DON'T MISS YOUR EXIT

At what point do you distinguish between what's real and what's fiction? You are headed nowhere going fast and you realize that you have been spinning your wheels.

Don't ever give your time away because you cannot get time back that has been wasted.

NOTES

NOTES

NOTES

NOTES

*SOME PEOPLE ARE HOLDING
GRUDGES AGAINST YOU FOR
THINGS THEY DID TO YOU.*

CHAPTER 6

There's a Power You Can Tap Into

When you are asking God to use you, do you know what you're asking him to do? I don't know about you, but if you've ever been to a place where you've been used, that's a painful place; that's a place that is uncomfortable. And sometimes we have to go to a place that's uncomfortable in order to see what God has in store for us. And sometimes we don't want to walk alone. If you ever find yourself feeling like you're all alone; like you're at a place where you really can't talk to people because they don't understand the mandate that's on your life. Then there's a place and times of uncomfortableness and you ask the Lord; Lord, why do you put me here? I don't know about you, but sometimes I have to ask him these questions. Lord, I know you called me and I know I am going to be true to the calling. But do I have to go through this, just to get an anointing? Some of you are going to understand what I'm saying. You ask yourself if you have to go through this, through the crushing of the oil in order to get the anointing. And his answer's going to be yes, because he is going to make sure that when you come out of this, as above, so is below; no matter how high you go, and no matter how low you've been; you still will be able to proclaim his name and you will change, and you will be able to say, no matter how low you have to go, you will bless the Lord at all times and his praise shall continually be in your mouth.

Sometimes you are going to be mocked. And I hope you have a heart that breaks for the lost. When someone mocks your faith, I hope that the first thing that comes to your mind is the thought the person really doesn't know Jesus. And you have to understand that some people really don't know him. They have heard of him, but they don't know him. And sometimes it can be overwhelming to you to know there are people out there that do not know him. But you have to understand that your hope is in him. And if you can give the lost hope, then you have done what he has asked you to do.

I can recall when I decided to put my life down and follow Christ; I didn't have it all together. Even in the beginning of my marriage before we even got married, I didn't have it all together. I failed at a lot and I learned a lot. And it was in my failures that taught me what to do and what not to do. It taught me how to become a better me. And I know that sometimes as men and women, you think that whenever you fail…it breaks you, it paralyzes you, as I mentioned before. But the man and the woman of God that puts down his plans for his own life and picks up God's, that's a gift. And when the man or woman does that, they will tap into a strength that is far beyond the sum-total of their skill. It's going to be far beyond the sum-total of your experiences and your aspirations.

There's not a channel of power that you cannot tap into that God will not relinquish to you. Why? Because you are in a position of receiving and the desire is there. As I sit here on my front porch, the Holy Spirit is just speaking to me. There's a power that you can tap into. Have you heard the saying there's a place in God that the enemy cannot come. And in the midst of that place you have to understand, that that's your safe haven. You need to tap into that place sometimes, meditate and think, it could have gone in another direction. Sometimes when the cares of this world have overtaken you, and pride gets in your way. You need to understand that it isn't always others, sometimes it is us. We have to just be real, it is us sometimes. Will the real you come forth? Yeah, come forth the real you. Because pride comes before a great fall. You have to let your pride go. Whatever you are in need of you will never be able to get it or achieve it with your pride in the way.

You may have to ask others in order to seek direction. Some of us don't like to ask for anything; because we just believe we can conquer whatever; and maybe you can. But guess what, you're going to need someone in this life that has been where you are trying to go. You also have the ability to seek your answer in prayer. Call on a higher power, he's going to help you to be able to conquer anything that you ever need any challenges that comes your way, any altercations, any confrontations, you can do it best if you have him by your side. Trust and believe you can step out there, and that's exactly what you'll be out there by yourself. Will you stand having done all to stand? It's your call to take a positive stand also; to be found in one's place, to be standing in the place of knowing that God has called you to be and knowing that whatever comes your way that God is with you and carrying you.

NOTES

NOTES

NOTES

NOTES

CHAPTER 7

Falling In Love with the Process

Sometimes we see the facts of life and wonder which part of the play we take part in. And I'm here to tell you sometimes you have to be the author of your own play. You get to write how your life will end. No one gets to tell you how it's going to end. You speak what you want to see. And I'm here to tell you that whatever your heart's desire is you can become it, you can be it, and you can do it. You just have to put forth an effort. I know you have heard this time and time again. But if you never get started, you will never know what the end result will be.

Sometimes in life; and I keep referring back to life because life is worth living. And if you don't live your life, then you'll let somebody else live it for you and you'll be a part of living someone else's life in which you never intended. How can you be something that you never intended to be all because people try to tell you, who you are, who you're not, what you are going to become, what you're not going to become, what you can do, what you cannot do, what you can achieve, what you cannot achieve. You can become, do, and achieve anything you put your mind to; but most of the time, the association of people that you are around will actually channel your thinking. It's going to challenge your mindset. And most of the time, you're going to be just like the people that you're around. So if you're around great people then you're going to have great ideas. If you're around people that are always being negative and talking about everybody, and what they are doing, and what they are not doing; then that's going to rub off on you; because, you can only go as high as your elevator will take you. Okay, being a little comical here, but you are only going to go as far as the numbers on your elevator. How high do you want to go? How high do you want to soar? You can go as high as you want. But again sometimes the people in our lives; most of them; they do mean us well. But you have to understand you are not made like them. And they are not made like you. Therefore, do not expect anything out of them that's not in them. You are expecting people to do for you only what God can do. And, only what you can do for yourself. You should never be with your hand out expecting people to always give, give, give. You don't want to be that kind of person. You need to understand there is a balance in the relationships we have, whether it's a boyfriend and girlfriend or whether it's a co-worker. If they always buy you lunch and you never offered to buy them back, then that's a one-sided relationship. So you have to ask yourself, what kind of person do you want to be and what kind of relationship would you want people to give back to you. And the effort of that relationship I should say, because on this journey, it is not always about you.

Sometimes people will be so selfish, it's all about them. What can I get out of this? What can I, I, it's all about me. I will say that's the reason why I have been so blessed; is because I realize that I can't do anything by myself. You need a team of people around you, sometimes to support and encourage you. And if they're not, then you have to draw strength within yourself to know; hey you can do this yourself because you have been around great leaders, you have been around great people to inspire and encourage you. You can't always wait for somebody to row your boat, because some people in the boat are not rowing, they are eager to drop the anchor; they are putting a hole in your boat. And you've got to know the difference. You can't be so naive that you don't know how to discern people's spirits. Sometimes people will get offended with you because you decided to keep the course while they want to just galley and goof around. All they want to do is talk about what the world is doing and what it's not doing; when you did it twenty years ago. It's because they are not as spiritually mature as they should be. And sometimes it can aggravate you knowing the people around you are not mature. But you've got to let them grow to the mature level that you did because we all were once there. However; you can't always stay there, where it is comfortable, get out of your comfort zone, and step out of the boat like Peter did.

Sometimes you have to let your faith do the talking and the walking. I know sometimes it seems impossible, but how will you know if you don't try? You can't go by what somebody else tells you. You've got to try it yourself. Then you can make a declaration and say I know this works because I have tried it myself. And in the part of having a circle around you, make sure that you check that circle. You don't need a yes man or yes woman around you all the time. Make sure in the midst of that circle, whether it is small or big, they can strengthen you, and they want the best for you; not hating on you or being jealous of you; because if everybody is going to the same place then we are all going to get there; that's what I mean about having a circle around you. It's not that you need to be a people pleaser or that you have to have someone around you, sometimes it's good and refreshing to enjoy your own company; knowing you're okay being by yourself. Sometimes people are loners, and they don't want a bunch of people around them and I get that. But in the midst of you having people around you; make sure that you've got the right people around you that you can trust, and they can trust you. It will not do you any good to have people around you that don't want the best for you. Please make sure they have a prayer life. And they don't just talk it, okay. Sometimes people will say one thing but you check their action. Their actions say something else, because people are dealing with a lot of issues. And sometimes you become victim of circumstance. Have you ever been around someone, and you're like oh my God, why am I feeling like this? It's because you have entertained those spirits that you've been around. And if you're not strong enough, it's going to latch on to you. And before you know it, you're feeling down and depressed. Like oh my God, what is this that's trying to steal my joy. And then you try to be happy. You try to find joy in any situation. If you ever find yourself around people and all they see is negativity, and all they can see in others is negativity, I can assure they are not happy with themselves. You have found yourself trying to always uplift their spirit and yours, because they have literally drained you. This can come from a person that is an unhappy individual. Trust and believe me they are trying to take the attention off of themselves.

You have got to stop being around vision killers. Yes you have to stop being around vision killers. They are going to kill your vision because they don't have one for themselves. Sometimes it can stem from a lack of exposure. So, whatever you can make happen for others; you ought to be able to make happen for yourself. It's good to take advice from people that you trust, people that you believe in, and people that you saw that it happened in their life. You'd never ask a naked man to give you clothes. You wouldn't ask a blind man how to drive if he hasn't driven a car. Don't cheat yourself from going through the experience. Yes, he can tell you from what someone has told him. But he has never practiced it before. So logically thinking and realistically we have to stop this nonsense and putting our emotions and putting our faith into people that really don't care anything for you.

There's going to come a time when God is going to uncover peoples true colors, If you are spinning your wheels trying to become something, now that's good. You need to write that in the back of your notes. Stop spinning your wheels to become something and just be okay. You have to be it. And nobody can take away from you what you are; remember that, your mind is strong. Nobody can take away from you who you are. It's only if you are insecure that peoples' mindset can imply on you. If your mind is strong, then you know that you are strong and you can do and become all that you desire to be or become.

NOTES

NOTES

NOTES

NOTES

AND HE SAID TO ME, "MY GRACE IS SUFFICIENT FOR YOU, FOR MY STRENGTH IS MADE PERFECT IN WEAKNESS.

~~~2 CORINTHIANS 12:9 NKJV~~~

CHAPTER 8

You Are More than Enough

You are more than enough. Please know that I don't care what your past has dictated to you; I don't care what people have said that you are, yes, you may have done it, but that's not who you are. You may have did what they said, but that's not who you are, because God has already forgiven you, and you have forgiven yourself. And you cannot be victim of people's thoughts. You cannot be victim of people's ways.

People want to keep you down. The problem that I have and it isn't a big problem; but the problem that some of you will face is that you come from the same place other people have come from. But you're no longer there. You're going to catch it in a minute. Every time they see you they can't understand what you did. It's because you have decided to do something different with your life instead of allowing your past to dictate your future. You came from the same place that other people did, whether it was a small city or overcoming a temptation, but you are no longer there. That can be a concept of the way your mindset is. Kingdom minded people build people up; religion will tear people down. So you judge yourself and nobody else will have to.

IF YOU TOOK CARE OF YOUR OWN FIRST BEFORE YOU TAKE CARE OF SOMEONE ELSE YOU MAY GET THE ATTENTION YOU ARE SEEKING.

Okay, I'm also grateful to know that, I say this often… A moment of gratitude actually improves your attitude. You have to be grateful for everything that you have accomplished. Be grateful for anything and everything that someone has ever done or said towards you that was good, and even the accomplishments you have done yourself because people don't have to be kind. And when people are kind; when people are good, we need to have a grateful heart; you know to say, thank you, because people don't have to be good to you. There are some ruthless people out there and they do not have to be kind to you. And the mere fact that they are good to you and kind to you; we can have an attitude of being thankful.

Gratefulness and thankfulness will take you a long way. Ungrateful people complain about the one thing you have not done for them, instead of being grateful for the thousand things you have done. Don't invest your time and energy into people who think it's your obligation to cure their illness. It's okay to cancel your subscription. There may come a time in your life where Satan will use others to knock you off your A game. Pass the ball! Don't double dribble or foul out. It could cost you and the team the game. What are you saying? Never allow Satan to make you think they are for you, while the entire time they are plotting and discouraging others to do the same; trying to separate and divide. As a family, never allow anyone to favor one over the other. Let me leave a nugget for the marriage couples. Watch out for the strange fire that comes to like everything on your boyfriend/girlfriend and or husband/wife page; yet refuses to like or comment on your post knowing all the time they see it. How can they like your significant others' page knowing they are committed in a relationship or married? Some will call that trifling. There is nothing wrong with being cordial. But you need to know your place and know your role. You should never disrespect the other mate or spouse as well as your own. Put yourself in the other persons' shoes and act accordingly; respect what you expect. If you can pour that much attention into your significant other then you may reap the attention that you are searching for. And besides when you give more attention to another man or woman, more than you do your own, you are out of order. It's not that the person does not like you. It's that they will not allow, nor will they tolerate you or anyone else to disrespect them. It is called being and doing too much. Yes, it can make you want to dunk the ball and swing on the goal. However, you may have to pass the ball in order to get a better shot. You already know the opposing team came to win and have a plan up their sleeve as well. Watch as well as pray. They will make it seem to others that something is wrong with you. This will seem unfair but don't pay attention to the noise. The minute you become preoccupied and unfocused you will lose ground, and the enemy will come in like a flood. But my God will raise up a standard against him. Never allow the noise to get you off your A game so that you become ineffective. It is just a test, so do not get caught up in that web of reverse psychology. People will have you feeling some type of way about how they have treated you as though you have done something to them. It is a dangerous person who can never admit their faults and can see the faults in everyone else besides themselves. You have to pick and choose which battles are worth fighting. It is not how big the dog is in the fight as much as how much fight is in the dog.

Okay, know who you are; know that you are a good person, and know that you would help someone along the way. You are not the result of how people treat you. But you are the result of the total package of what you do to others and how you treat them. We must remember that we reap what we sow; so, try to have a mindset of exemplifying good morals and great character. Remember that you first have to take the tools and principles to work on you. Now go ahead ad drink a glass of water. Because I know that all of this may have been a hard pill to swallow.

NOTES

NOTES

NOTES

NOTES

FOR IT IS GOD WHO IS WORKING AMONG YOU BOTH THE WILLING AND THE WORKING FOR HIS GOOD PURPOSE.

~~~PHILIPPIANS 2:13 HCSB~~~

CHAPTER 9

Weathering the Storm

If your mind does not shift you will never be able to reach new places or different levels! Some may be waiting on the elevator and it seems stuck on one floor. Take the steps and keep it moving. Some things may not come to you easily. You have to put the work in; whatever you put in is the result of what's been happening. The minute we don't see results we think God has failed us. But the reality is we did just enough to get by. So how long will you wait for the elevator to come? Take the steps while weathering the storm. Stay encouraged, there's a message in the storm. I pray this blesses you from life's storms. You are precious in His sight.

There's a season change of course but don't misinterpret it. Remember you will always take yourself with you. So don't be your own storm where we need to send in an emergency relief just to get you to safety. Prepare yourself to weather any storm so you won't be caught off guard. If you don't have enough Word of God and a prayer life you will self-destruct.

I woke up this morning and God spoke these words to me. In life when people's plans don't go the way they intended, they will separate in hopes that others will think something is wrong with you, but in reality it is you just saw their hidden motives. Just remember no matter where you go you will always carry yourself. Everyone wants something for nothing these days. But not today, you must pay the price just like others had to, there are no shortcuts.

You may be good, until someone challenges you to reach beyond your limitations or to reach beyond what you can do for yourself. You are excited and reflect what others are doing but you are still in the same situation that you were in one to five years ago. Don't get alarmed when you are made to feel uncomfortable about lack. You can't always get over on people and paint a picture like someone did you wrong. No wisdom used then no lesson learned. Don't be the person that knows everything to where it becomes a repeat pattern or learned behavior.

NOTES

NOTES

NOTES

NOTES

*IT IS BETTER TO FORGIVE
AND FORGET THAN TO
RESENT AND REMEMBER.*

CHAPTER 10

When You Realize Life is Worth Living

There's a certain calmness that comes when knowing you earned a second chance and for most of us a third and fourth chance to change your pattern of life. Some things you just have to live through to pass over it, to start all over again. Some walks of life can't be taught, however, on the other side it can. If we would have only yielded to his voice, our lives would be so different. But in most cases we didn't, and as a result we are the part of the life we created.

You may be asking the question, where do I go from here; it's your own desires that are shaping you and sending off those alerts in your mind and intellect that give you zeal to move forward.

Have you ever asked yourself why I like what I like? It's only then when you accept who you are that you can accept you. I've never been a person that was easily persuaded. My mind was strong and if I did something it was because I chose to do so. We can't meander in life blaming others for the decisions we made. I taught my sons to do right because it is right and it will turn out alright. Behind every decision we all make there will be consequences, good or bad. But for most of us life didn't pass us by, we stopped believing in ourselves. You cannot wait for the approval of others as if time was going to stop just for you to get it right. It's ok to mark time just don't waste it, because we can never get it back.

When you are in the phase of life of trying to figure you out, that's not the time to put your life in the hands of others. If people are not sure who they are, why would you put that much power into someone that's trying to figure it out. Once you fall in love with you then you can walk in confidence and face this world head on. Prayer is the key and faith undoubtedly unlocks all the closed doors that you once faced in doubt. Get up, believe in yourself, and remember the only person you are comparing and competing with is yourself to be better than you were yesterday. Stop letting your emotions over power your intelligence.

Life has a way of making us or breaking us. However, it's what you do after the fact that will determine if you stand back up. Never allow pride to render your downfall. The mistake we make is thinking we can handle what was meant for us to learn as opposed to wearing it. You can't wear something that no longer fits. Take it off! The struggle will come knowing you took them off while others never saw your inward change. The heart was meant to pump blood and never to get involved with everything and everyone's matters.

And when you make the decision to becoming a better you, the spirits and all of his cousins have to let go! Take off some things like pride, hatred, and un-forgiveness just to name a few. So, remember when the new you stands up to have to feed your inner man with positive thinking; it doesn't matter what you've done, we serve a God that loves us; in-spite of our shortcomings. Yeah, you may have done it, but that's not who you are. It's not what they call you baby, but what you answer to. You are blessed and highly favored. You are the sons and daughters of the most Holy. So will the real you step forward? The challenge you will have is not knowing and believing the change, but in receiving it. What's not believable by you will never be achievable. Your least worry is knowing where you came from as opposed to where you are going. Don't allow the opinion of others to set your course of life; they have no clue who you are becoming. It's not your fault they can't fathom how you are doing what you are doing because you all came from the same place.

Only if they knew the tears you cried and the days on your knees praying and trusting God through the process. They called you peculiar and you were. If you have ever been below and God brings you above I promise you there will be a grateful, thankful spirit working through you. Only you know what He did for you and only you know how long it took. You can't get caught up in the Who's Who, but whosoever will let him come. I myself am part of the "whosoever" will club. There are no monthly fees, there are no annual prescriptions. All you need is a yes, a willing heart, and thankful spirit. Send me, I will go.

This is where you make a declaration, and shout it on the mountain top; that you don't owe your past an apology as much as you owe your future an opportunity. I'm coming out with my hands up. Praising him for everything he blocked and everything he allows you to go through and come out! Won't he do it! Your best days are before you. Live your best life.

Make peace with all mankind and live your best life owing no man but to love him.

Go out and inspire someone with your life in hopes they will do the same. We are only the sum-total of our being, so make life count. What are you doing to help make a change in another person's life? Sometimes we have to be to others what we so desire others to be to us. Be the change you want to see. It won't hurt you to be kind.

People are looking for genuine people, not people that always want something for nothing. Have you ever been around people that pull from your account not necessarily money but never making a deposit; run quick, fast and in a hurry. They are called parasites or opportunists, and will bleed you dry. Until they have an encounter with the master of this thing we call life they can never appreciate and value you or your gift. You cannot hold people accountable for what they truly are not capable of doing or being. Other peoples' standards are not the same as yours. If you are not careful you will be the one hurting the most, because you are wanting and desiring something from them that can only come from God. Love people where they are but never allow them to make you feel inferior because they can't discipline themselves to make a change in their life in hopes of being a better person. Until a person is sick and tired they will continue to do the same thing they were doing five years ago expecting different results.

Are you awake? The hardest part is getting started. You can't talk about what you are not willing to face and take a chance on. People just don't wake up with dreams being fulfilled or dropped out of the sky. It takes work, long hours and having a strategy in order to execute the plan. You have to see your ending in the beginning. Never forget why you started.

You can't be hating and jealous of a person that decided to get up and go after their dreams. Yes, we can talk about it but we must have corresponding actions. Now on the other side of the quadrant the measurements will require a greater source of longitude and latitude that's factor in the direction you are going which is up. What requires God require God. Faith without works is dead. Don't wait on God to do what you are capable of doing. Your mindset is a good place to start. People can only conceive from their perspective. So stop worrying about how someone may view you. That's no longer your problem. You have what it takes. Are you prepared for the journey? Know when to change and be ok with it, especially if it's making you a better you.

NOTES

NOTES

NOTES

NOTES

IF WE ARE NOT CONTINUALLY FED WITH GOD'S WORD, WE WILL STARVE SPIRITUALLY.

CHAPTER II

Matters of the Heart

My beloved our hearts were designed to pump blood and not allow it to be involved in every matter. When you realize that you have what it takes, and your heart is still pumping; and I repeat when you realize that you have what it takes and your heart is still pumping, then your perspective of life will shift. You have another chance of picking up the pieces and putting them back together because you know where they fit and who you are as a result.

Some things are only meant to be a bridge to bring you over. Don't get so stuck in life's disappointment that you never pass your past. Never allow the missing piece of someone else's imperfections to make you second guess and question your ability to perform. You can live life or let life pass you by. It's just like a sponge, what's in you has got to come out when it's under pressure.

I want to share with you that when life presented itself unseemly to me, it almost took my breath. The woman that birthed me, raised me, and imparted into me the lady I have become, is now needing me to walk by her side, assuring that she doesn't fall or lose hope. When I see her health declining right in front of my eyes, that's painful. I'm sure some of you reading this, has witnessed this part also in your life. When you are at the peak of your career and your mom tells you, "I don't want to be a burden." I looked at her. And I said, "As long as I am capable and well able, you will never have anything to worry about." And with the help of God, prayers, and my family, she is still hanging on.

Wearing a lot of hats can sometimes be overwhelming, especially if you are not equipped or called. Therefore make sure you don't forget which one you are called in order to be effective and productive. You don't want to have so much going on that you don't have a balanced life. Know when to unplug and take time out for family and most importantly yourself. Don't feel bad when you do, it's all a part of regrouping.

NOTES

NOTES

NOTES

NOTES

CHAPTER 12

Be a Bridge to Help Someone Over

What you allow to define you will be your point of happiness. Learn to celebrate small victories. If you set your goals and achieve them, then celebrate. Don't ever get to a point that what use to matter becomes just another thing on your to do list. You will miss out on the gratitude of fulfilling something that you wanted to achieve. Life just doesn't happen, goals just don't get accomplished, and dreams just don't come true. There's a period in your life called perseverance, dedication and hard work just to name a few.

Sometimes you have to be the coach to your own team. Encourage yourself and inspire others to do the same. You can't stop now! Get up, show up, and put your all in towards your finished goal. You have the ability to set the pace and get a strategy in place. Listen to me, it's not just going to happen, you have to put the work in. Plant your seed and wait for the return. Once the seed is planted, buried, watered then it starts to germinate. Life begins when you take the time to cultivate what you have planted.

Have you ever asked yourself what is required in order to live your best life? How you measure and define your life will determine the degree it is capable of achieving. You were created for what? You desire to do what? You feel your best when you have accomplished what? These are some of the questions that we ponder over waiting to see and get the results. This is a start of creating something in you that you sense it's there. You just haven't figured out how to get it out or how to orchestrate it from a place where you truly are. Be honest, be real with yourself because the only person that needs to recognize where you are is you.

If you have to pick up the pieces sugar, then pick them up and let's start putting them back together. You may have to redefine normal and that's okay because some things can never go back to the way it was. You may find yourself uncomfortable and afraid of what you see or should I say what you don't see.

Put your all in and this time, believe in yourself. You will never go where you think you are not worthy of going. Yes, you are going to make mistakes from time to time, but learn the lesson in order to find the blessing. It's waiting on you because now you know! You may not know quite yet what your best life looks like or what it doesn't look like. You have found hope again and now your strength and your confidence have caught up with you. Don't waste time wondering what you could have been by now. Focus on who you are and the masterpiece you are becoming. It's just like fine wine, it gets better in time.

As you go through your day, remember the triggers that put you in a place of locked down frustration and worry. So you won't allow those issues to intrude in your thought process or your day. You have the power now to control your thoughts and your intellect. Don't waste your energy on anything that's not going to produce a positive return. If you've ever been through a dark or low place and you finally get enough wind to start again, then you cannot allow anything or anyone to set you back. You have to remember how long it took you to get to a rested place; therefore you can't allow anyone to disturb your peace. Keep believing and trusting the process. You win this time and your best days are just ahead.

YOUR CAREER IS WHAT
YOU PAID FOR AND YOUR
CALLING IS WHAT YOU ARE
MADE FOR.

NOTES

NOTES

NOTES

NOTES

"SET YOUR AFFECTION ON THINGS ABOVE, NOT ON THINGS ON THE EARTH."

~~~COLOSSIANS 3:2~~~

Bibliography

Quotespaper.com

About The Author

Shelby Kellam has served in the ministry for over 25 years alongside her husband, Bishop Reginald Kellam. Those who work with her in ministry affectionally call her "Lady Kellam". Lady Kellam truly has a servant's heart filled with compassion for others. She is known for her powerful, life-changing, and prophetic messages wrapped in grace and elegance.

Her ministry transcends racial barriers and denominations and has affected many throughout the United States. The prophetic evangelistic call on her life has afforded her opportunities to minister nationally and globally. Whether it's in the boardroom, office or church, Lady Kellam works diligently to find balance between her evangelistic calling and commitment as a ministry leader. She is the First Lady of

Friendship Missionary Baptist Church and her personal life as a professional entrepreneur, life coach, wife, and mother.

Lady Kellam is a native of Rockingham County, N.C., a small farming community. But later moved to the city of Greensboro, N.C. She earned a Bachelor's in Business Administration with concentration in Management and currently is one of the CEO's of Head 2 Toe Boutique and Owner of A2Z Custom Designs T-shirts, currently located in Kernersville, N.C.

Arise, Shine; for thy light is come, and the glory of the Lord is risen upon thee (Isaiah 60:1); is her favorite scripture. She believes that with God all things are possible.

www.ingramcontent.com/pod-product-compliance
Lightning Source LLC
Chambersburg PA
CBHW021241090426
42740CB00006B/629